Words by the Water

JOHNS HOPKINS: *Poetry & Fiction*

John T. Irwin, General Editor

ALSO BY WILLIAM JAY SMITH (a selection)

POETRY

Poems

Celebration at Dark

Poems 1947–1957

The Tin Can and Other Poems

New and Selected Poems

The Traveler's Tree: New and Selected Poems

Collected Poems: 1939–1989

The World below the Window: Poems 1937–1997

The Cherokee Lottery: A Sequence of Poems

The Girl in Glass: Love Poems

Laughing Time: Collected Nonsense

Birds and Beasts

CRITICISM AND MEMOIRS

The Spectra Hoax

The Streaks of the Tulip: Selected Criticism

Army Brat: A Memoir

Dancing in the Garden: A Bittersweet Love Affair with France

TRANSLATIONS

Poems of a Multimillionaire by Valery Larbaud

Selected Writings of Jules Laforgue

Collected Translations: Italian, French, Spanish, Portuguese

The Moral Tales of Jules Laforgue

(with Leif Sjöberg) *Agadir* by Artur Lundkvist

(with Leif Sjöberg) *Wild Bouquet: Nature Poems* by Harry Martinson

Words by the Water

WILLIAM JAY SMITH

The Johns Hopkins University Press BALTIMORE

This book has been brought to publication with the generous assistance of the Albert Dowling Trust.

The Johns Hopkins University Press
2715 North Charles Street
Baltimore, Maryland 21218-4363
www.press.jhu.edu

Library of Congress
Cataloging-in-Publication Data

Smith, William Jay, 1918–
Words by the water / William Jay Smith.
    p. cm. — (Johns Hopkins, poetry and fiction)
ISBN-13: 978-0-8018-9064-2 (acid-free paper)
ISBN-13: 978-0-8018-9065-9 (pbk. : acid-free paper)
ISBN-10: 0-8018-9064-0 (acid-free paper)
ISBN-10: 0-8018-9065-9 (pbk. : acid-free paper)
I. Title.
PS3537.M8693W66 2008
811'.54—dc22   2008013741

A catalog record for this book is available
from the British Library.

Special discounts are available for bulk purchases of this book. For more information, please contact Special Sales at 410-516-6936 or specialsales@press.jhu.edu.

To Sonja

CONTENTS

AUTHOR'S NOTE

The three poems, "Of Islands," "On His Dark Bed," and "Reflection," which now form part of a new poetic sequence, were written in 1942 on the atoll of Palmyra, where I was stationed for five months as a U.S. Navy communications officer. Although I had published poems in national magazines in high school and college, it was there that I feel my career as a poet actually began. I developed at the time a sense of purpose and direction that is with me still and that informs, I hope, the other poems in this book. I have reprinted eight poems from the previous selection of my work, *The World below the Window* (1998), and two lyrics from *The Cherokee Lottery* (2000), but all the other poems here are new and uncollected. Three of the ten translations are new and the others are from out-of-print collections. I have included "Oxford Doggerel," my view of Oxford in 1947, because it has been of some interest and is not available elsewhere.

I am grateful to Robert Andrew Parker for the illustration in this book.

Miklós Vajda assisted me with the Hungarian translations, and the late Leif Sjöberg with the Swedish.

Words by the Water

O Love, O Love, these oceans vast

— HERMAN MELVILLE

PRELUDE

All that I see must in my sight become
So sparkling clear that waves of vision break
Upon my eye as on some coral-comb
The wild Pacific . . . and I summon Blake
To guide my thoughts beyond that curling foam
As he would lambs to pasture by a lake
And leave them frolicking till Kingdom Come.

And all that now is ill will then be well,
will then be well;
And all that now is ill will then be well.

The Atoll

THE ATOLL

An island is all one can ever know
    And all that can ever be
Though part of a vast archipelago
    Rooted in the sea.

It is all one feels, all one finds,
    All that the heart lays bare:
An atoll formed (the waking mind's)
    Open on endless air.

OF ISLANDS

Of all the islands sailing down the west,
Of islands sailing north and south and east,
It is not islands you remember best—
Or better, have forgotten least.

It is not land, the quick, sure touch of trees,
Not all the lusty continent which sense reveals,
Which floats upon the mind immense with ease,
And steals away as quick as darkness steals.

It is not islands. It is less than islands,
Land still land until at once you see
You have come upon a calm, enclosed lagoon
And earth in its entirety:

And since it is an interim of sea and air,
Even as islands ultimately are,
And the waves are clouds which crawl back up the sky
To overtake a star:

Then even if the land is land no man can mend,
Which salt nor sand nor star can clean,
This is the island which our lives defend
Where life must end, and death put forth its green.

NOTE: PALMYRA

The island that I was prepared to defend was Palmyra, a coral atoll a thousand miles southwest of Hawaii and 350 miles north of the equator, at almost the exact center of the Pacific Ocean. The U.S. Navy took it over in 1940, and after the Japanese attack on Pearl Harbor, it became an important airbase, the first stop for planes to refuel on their way south. In May 1942, at the Battle of Midway, the U.S. Navy, having broken the Japanese code, defeated the Japanese and kept them from occupying Hawaii. At that time there were only a few hundred men stationed on Palmyra, but they managed with their five-inch gun battery to drive off an attacking Japanese submarine.

I arrived shortly afterward, a naval communications officer, and remained for five months.

It was at night on Palmyra, with water on every side and the phosphorescent breakers of that vast ocean pounding the reef and the Southern Cross above at my fingertips, that I came to know the terrifying beauty of being at what seemed then the edge of this earth.

ON HIS DARK BED

He who has felt on his dark bed
    The pressure of the tides
Finds sunlight ebbing round his head,
    Morning on all sides.

Like all heaven the hound will eat from his hand,
    And the wave like a newborn foal;
Manes engulfing a green island,
    Lions court his soul.

Lions that walk the yellow sand
    On the blood of morning fed;
And he who wakes finds light, his land;
    Darkness, fleeing, fled.

REFLECTION

*Sometimes after decoding messages all night long, I would
awaken in the afternoon on my bunk, thinking of those Polynesian
mariners in their outrigger canoes who were probably the first to
visit this and other islands in the Pacific.*

As from a rainbow, the canoe
Is launched on a lagoon
Below the temple steps.

Under fronded boughs,
Lizard-blue, the water
Licks the white shore,

And the trades blow calm.
Upon my wall, the shadow of a giant palm
Branch bends, a claw, a hand,

Like all reality in reflection
Caught, out of time, beyond waves' hum,
And wind's delirium.

Rage, wild water. For the world
Rides my eye, as evermore
The canoe its element.

THE GARDEN

I knew that I had arrived in paradise:
The island was a garden but not a garden like Eden
with one terrace above another so high
that no deluge could ever touch it.
No, this was a Persian garden walled in by ocean;
from the edge of the lagoon, I stepped into a sparkling world
of water-flowers with fish like strips of rainbow
darting among enormous flowerbeds,
clusters of purple coral stalks
each ending in a tiny golden ear of corn,
a kernel shielding a living creature there inside.

Paradise is an island, the Hopi Indians claimed
but surely they meant one with ample water, hills, and trees.
Palmyra offered all these things:
The water on all sides was also in the air
and rain that fell each day was clear and cool,
refreshing all it touched and making greener the island's green.

Water was everywhere, but where were the hills?
I stood on the greenest hill one could imagine—
the coral-encrusted rim of an extinct volcano
resting on the ocean floor—and standing on its edge
I gazed down on even greener hills from which all life had come.

And the trees? Perched on the coral rim was a swaying line
of palm trees and thick shrubbery that gave the blue lagoon
a fine green crown. Below the coral edge nested
hundreds of booby birds, as clumsy as clowns
until they rose majestically
above the flocks of terns adrift on the cooling breeze
that swept in from the sea.

When clouds gathered and the rain began to fall,
I parted it, a bead-curtain,
to peer into a blue-green, rainbow-edged world,
an earthly paradise,
beyond time, constantly refreshed and reforming.

THE FLIGHT

"Come," the Captain said, "let me show you
how this place looks from the air."
And I followed him to the monoplane, the little "cat"
waiting at the end of the runway.
We strapped ourselves in—he in front
and me behind—and soon the propeller began to turn
and we were off into space,
leaving the atoll and its blue lagoon below.

A sputtering of the engine,
a strong smell of oil, the constant swirl of air
over our faces, and the incessant shaking
of the plane, the voice of the radioman
on the island crackling through the static—
I lost all sense of time.
How long had we been up? Ten minutes,
fifteen, twenty, forty-five? . . . I was nodding
and slipping off into another world
when suddenly, loud and clear,
the Captain spoke to bring me back.
To the radioman he said, "We'd better find
our way down soon because we are running
out of gas." . . . I clearly saw at once
the beginning of our end.

                    And it was then
that the voices began to reach me—
faint at first, and fluttering
mothlike through consciousness—
but gradually thickening, growing more distinct
and resonant—until they all got through to me
just as they had originally
when they had come from that other plane
that was trying desperately to find our island . . .
and were soon swallowed up by the sea.

How long had we been up? My whole life flew by in seconds,
and I knew that I was ready to answer
those voices rising from their deep well . . .
I would find those who had been unable to find me.
I would reach them easily now
wherever it was they had lain so long in wait.

I was prepared for our end, for the slap of the cold wave
and everything beyond . . . but first I turned aside
one final time, and—
miracle of miracles—
a bead-curtain of rain cut through the air
to reveal an open segment of sky
and below it an atoll and a blue lagoon.

The island garden flew up to greet us—
all its perfumes and water-flowers encircling our faces—
as the plane brought us back to the coral strip
where great waves broke on the world's edge,
and standing there at the reef's very tip
I found the mind's ever-present clear image
of that sleek tropic tree,
one slender fronded branch
projected into infinity.

NOTE: THE ATOLL

The atoll of Palmyra, which is a mile and a half long and half a mile wide, consists of a string of fifty-two small islets formed by the growth of coral on the rim of an extinct submerged volcano. It supports three times as many coral species as are found in all Hawaii and three times the number of species reported in the entire Caribbean. When the U.S. Navy took over Palmyra in 1940, it was the property of the Fullard-Leo family of Honolulu. In 1947 the family took its claim of ownership to the U.S. Supreme Court, and when it won, the navy gave up possession of the island. Over the years many offers to purchase the island were made, one proposing its use as a dump for nuclear waste and another to make it a gigantic gambling casino. But the family refused all offers until 2000, when it accepted that of the Nature Conservancy, and the island was then designated a U.S. National and Wild Life Refuge. Then Secretary of the Interior Bruce Babbitt, who called it "a jewel of America's coral reefs," said that it "should be protected from exploitation and be a place where future generations can for all time marvel at the pristine wonders of the tropical seas."

The supreme irony, of course, is that global warming, for which humanity is now recognized as largely responsible, is causing the death of the coral that built up this island. And so we may one day send the paradise we have saved back into the ocean from which it came.

The Hunt

WILLOW WOOD

The wood of the willow tree has long been a
component of artificial legs.

The soldier spoke up and said, "God bless the willows!
On willow wood I walk: come with me down
this lovely country lane outside of town."
The soldier spoke up and spoke for the other fellows.

"I lost both legs," he said, "in a roadside blast;
they swirled off into the sand where I'd come to fight,
and follow me now when I awake at night
and walk as in a dream far into the past . . .

"And walk to the edge of my youth where weeping willows
brush the cold spring water clear and sweet,
where I kick and swim and cut through summer heat
in a burst of joy with all the other fellows.

"The years go by, and still those willows bend
above that spring moss-rimmed by memory,
and in reflection weep, but not for me,
but for a world whose wars will never end."

INVITATION TO GROUND ZERO

Into the smoldering ruin now go down:
and walk where once she walked and breathe the air
she breathed that final day on the burning stair
and follow her, beyond the fleeing crowds,
into the fire, and through the climbing clouds.

Into the smoldering ruin now go down:
and find, in ashes bright as hammered tin,
a buried bone-white naked mannequin
that flung from some shop window serves to bind
her body, and its beauty, to your mind.

CONTEMPLATION OF CONSPIRACY

Where the table-leg projects into the yellow autumn
    sunlight
like the poor premise of an argument,
the plotters gather, rotting wood at a creek's end
tirelessly planning the devastation of the spirit,
wiring the heart for a final explosion.

Where can they lead you but over the bridges of beetroot
into the country of spiders?

Do not follow them to their camp pitched in a cranny;
bring your fist down hard on the table . . .
                 and send them flying.

THE POOR PEACOCK AND THE RICH PEACOCK

*James MacNeill Whistler was discharged in 1853 from West Point for his
failure in chemistry. "Had silicon been a gas, I would have been a major-
general," he said later. In 1877 Whistler brought suit in London against John
Ruskin, who had attacked his paintings, and although he won, the cost of
the suit left him bankrupt. He retired for a short while to Venice. On his
return to London, he executed the paintings for the Peacock Room in the
house of F. R. Leyland, which include studies of the Poor Peacock and the
Rich Peacock.*

The Poor Peacock never had a chance:
At a young age, he was thrown out of West Point
and it was downhill after that.
His feathers faded, and he dragged his tail, a rusty rake,
through the obfuscating mud;
he lit a match to its ragged spots
to keep them from his creditors when he declared bankruptcy.
He was last seen on the edge of a canal in Venice,
weeping into the water that had turned a sickening green
like poor patches of memory.

The Rich Peacock, on the other hand, flourished from the start:
he was born with panache.
He couldn't wait to rip off his West Point
uniform; he cut it into blue strips
that he pasted on canvas; its chevrons he fashioned
into streaks of moonlight.
The resulting "Nocturnes" were framed
and displayed in all the important museums;
the spots of his tail multiplied like the capitals of the world
and became increasingly incandescent.
At about this time he began his studies in black and gold
and laid plans for his Peacock Room.

"Come to the window," said the Rich Peacock, "it is getting dark,
and, with any luck, you will see what I see,
which is fabulous."

PERFECT LIVES: PORTRAITS

WINE MERCHANT

I drink to you, and as the dark wine
touches my lips, it calls up the vineyards
on the far-off misty slopes of my boyhood.
The Greeks were right to say there is no such thing
as a short life or a long life;
there is just the life you have,
the life you have been given.
That life has a pattern, a curve all its own,
as mine has had, and that life is perfect.

MOTHER

Age has cut furrows in my face
like those on the head of a cabbage.
I love the notion that children are born in cabbage leaves;
I see mine dancing there in all the green joy of their youth.
But at night the pain that furrows my face
divides my sleep: my head is severed from my body,
a cabbage, split through with a knife.

DANCER

A monarch butterfly crosses my dream
and before me, in gold and black, the tall grass divides.
I enter a clearing where blue-black earth
crumples like velvet as my bare feet move over it.
The reeds form a bead-curtain I part
with my breath, and every step I take is ecstasy.
I embody the precision that creates movement,
and, by moving, I become the light
that gives life to the world.

RIDDLES

for Daniel Hoffman

1.

Its rings record lost kingdoms, ancient wars;
through raging fires it stood and bears the scars,
yet climbs the mountainside to touch the stars.

2.

Green fountain which upon cool gravel played,
umbrella open over checkered shade,
great wheel of life with black spokes death-decayed,
gray hollow chunks that wet green flames invade.

3.

Pocket it: how rare and colorless a rose!
Direction keeps, and yet no destination knows.

4.

In wild, green-ruffled dress with plangent sound,
the dancer tosses, luring men around
the sleepy shoals where some have gone aground.

5.
Swan-haven
       Swan-light
Bright day
       Blue night
Gold arrow
       Clear air
Nowhere
       Everywhere

6.

A goad to some, to others but a toy;

painful to give but simple to destroy,

it has you by the throat—what pain, what joy!

1. Sequoia 2. Elm tree 3. Compass 4. Bell-buoy 5. Love 6. Life

THE ARTIST AND THE ARENA

The aerialist, about to sneeze,
    with pure poetic art,
looks gravely down from his trapeze
    on the dark arena of the heart.

In for the fun and out for the sights,
    in T-shirts, jeans, and slacks,
the disaffected Troglodytes
    concentrically relax.

"Art demands a careful balance
    for its reverent release:
Bless you bless you bless you bless you—*Que
    Dieu vous bénisse!*"

The deft performer, with a lurch
    from that appointed place,
tumbles from his celestial perch
    into eternal space.

In for the fun and out for the sights,
    in T-shirts, jeans, and slacks,
the disaffected Troglodytes
    arch their anxious backs.

Art that has seen far better days
    dispenses with applause
and one who only lived to please
    withdraws for no known cause.

THE HUNT

Each vowel black and white with silver sound,
each consonant, a coil of golden fleece
that's hunted over russet-colored ground—
chorale by Bach and painting by Matisse,
this language, life . . . Those hunting horns resound
so high up there you'd think they would release
the very sun itself the mountains round,
and penetrate deep valleys till they cease.

These words, this world; and all one sees and hears.
Think how, as if through time, the hunters ride
above the curling clouds while morning clears
and brings them breathless down the mountainside:
think how the dark divides to take their spears,
how in each poem life is justified.

The Deer and the Dachshund

LIGHT VERSE AND SATIRE

The deer and the dachshund are one.

—Wallace Stevens, "Loneliness in Jersey City"

DACHSHUNDS

The Dachshund leads a quiet life
    Not far above the ground:
He takes an elongated wife,
    They travel all around.

They leave the lighted metropole;
    Nor turn to look behind
Upon the headlands of the soul,
    The tundras of the mind.

They climb together through the dusk
    To ask the Lost-and-Found
For information on the stars
    Not far above the ground.

The Dachshunds seem to journey on:
    And following them, I
Take up my monocle, the Moon,
    And gaze into the sky.

Pursuing them with comic art
    Beyond a cosmic goal,
I see the whole within the part,
    The part within the whole;

See planets wheeling overhead,
    Mysterious and slow,
While Morning buckles on his red,
    And on the Dachshunds go.

AUTHOR, AUTHOR

Poet-playwright, bear in mind
Posterity may not be kind;
Nothing very much endures
And what you write may not be yours.
Even Shakespeare, should he waken,
Will find that he was Francis Bacon,
And Molière, whom many praise,
Will learn that Corneille wrote his plays.

Literary is a work very difficult to do.—Julia Moore

There is no record that Julia Moore, the Sweet Singer of Michigan (1847–1920), ever appeared in a music hall, but if she had, she might have answered her critics with these words:

> When little Libby choked on a piece of beef
> And no one there could offer her relief
> And the poor dear thing dropped dead like an autumn leaf
> They came from far and wide
> To mourn at her graveside
> Her mother and her dad
> Her sisters and her brothers
> They all stood there so sad
> And so did many others
> But who was there but me
> To compose an elegy?
> And so while their tears flowed
> I wrote my famous ode
> "To little Libby who choked on a piece of beef."

Oh, the literary life is very hard,
And there's truly never been a just reward
For anyone who's born to be a bard.

> Some people think that writing
> Is terribly exciting,
> And more tempting and inviting
> Than bearbaiting or cockfighting.
> Let them keep on ravin'
> About the Bard of Avon,
> But take a tip from Me,
> Composing poetry
> Like splitting a split-pea
> Can be pure agony—

And with the critic's arrows I am scarred;
Oh, the literary life is very hard.

My husband is a dreadful man who drinks
And from responsibility he shrinks
And when he drinks he throws away
His money each payday
And so to make ends meet
And to keep me off the street
I have taken up my pen
And I write of drunken men
And many of my lines
Are of miners trapped in mines
Of the child who swallowed acid
Or fell into Lake Placid.
The man who's lost at sea
Or is hit by a falling tree
Or dies drinking poisoned tea
I record in poetry
I publish poems everywhere I can—
I'm Julia Moore, Sweet Singer of Michigan.

Oh, the literary life is very hard
And there's truly never been a just reward
For anyone who's born to be a bard.

It may seem rather grand
When you are named George Sand
And you can put on pants
But then she lived in France.
Out here in Kalamazoo
They watch each thing you do:
On porches people rocking,

With tongues like shotguns cocking,
Call my loving verses shocking
And "the blues of a bluestocking."

Oh, the literary life is very hard
And there's truly never been a just reward
For anyone who's born to be a bard.

The one reward for me
Will be immortality.
When Julia Moore is dead
And I'm buried in my glory
Those critics will be sorry
For the nasty things they said.
Posterity will point a loving finger
At Michigan's Sweet Singer,
At Julia Moore who's gone to her reward.

Oh, the literary life is very hard
And there's truly never been a just reward
For anyone who's born to be a bard.

That life was pretty tirin'
Even for Lord Byron,
Who was a man of iron.
It was the death of Keats,
Who coughed blood like pickled beets,
But it keeps me off the streets—

Oh, the literary life is very hard!

EPITAPHS

A SMALL WINNER

He always played his hand close to his chest;
And, leading with a heart, he did his best;
His best was very rarely good enough.
Yet none but Death, the Dealer, called his bluff.

A SMALL DOG

*A Lhasa apso that died fighting with a Saint Bernard
on the coast of Maine*

Here Fearless lies: with Asian pride,
Longhaired and small, by the Oceanside,
He took up the challenge, fought, and died;
Now hear his bark in the rising tide.

ON THE BANKS OF THE MISSISSIPPI

Memories of a Missouri boyhood

Old MacDonald had a farm
    A long time ago,
Before we had the School of Charm
    With an ee - i - ee - i - O

And on that farm he had a tire
    Hung from an oak as a swing.
Come, swing (ting-a-ling) and talk by wire
    Through tin cans on a string.

Hello, up there to the house on the hill,
    Hello to the house in the tree
Hello to the bird with the busy bill
    And the song like a door key.

Hello to the hill, hello to the star,
    May apple and wild rose,
The fireflies trapped in the Mason jar,
    The corn in long neat rows.

Hello to the dog the color of cream,
    Hello to the charcoal cat,
The crawfish caught in a muddy stream
    With strips of bacon fat.

Hello and good-bye to the little Ford cars
    That into their graveyard go:
They go to bed with our movie stars,
    Rin-tin-tin, Clara Bow.

Hello down there to the pink barber poles,
    To the band that marched on the green,
To those bittersweet paths and dark sinkholes
    Where Indian lean-tos lean.

Hello to the river that overflowed'
    Its broad mud flats in the spring
And lifted farmhouses off the dirt road,
    The toys of a mad brown king.

Old MacDonald had a farm;
    Wind and rain and snow
Never do the slightest harm:
    Hello! Hello! Hello!

OXFORD DOGGEREL

for the Rhodes Scholar Class of 1947

Memory is a dog that lies down where it pleases.
—Cees Nooteboom, *Rituals*

Memory is a dog that lies down where it pleases:
Into cracks and crannies of the past it squeezes,
Recrosses bridges you long ago crossed
And sniffs out places you thought were lost.
It races up mountains and paddles through waves,
Explores old graveyards and digs up graves.
On beaches, in basements, on cliffs, and in towers
It curls up with trivia and dozes for hours . . .
We gathered in Oxford from near and far,
The first Rhodes Scholars after the War,
A diversified and seasoned lot,
In that historic, special spot,
Some fresh from college, some retreads,
War veterans and newlyweds,
Since first we gazed on Oxford spires,
Untouched by fumes and factory fires,
Thirty-six years have now gone by.
And where will Memory, that dog, lie?
Beside what bent and blasted tree?
These are the bones it left with me . . .

Postwar Oxford—what was it like?
Each cold gray morning your bride on her bike
Would cycle off with her ration card,
Eager for some delicious reward,
A gourmet treat, a trifle, a truffle,
And what would she find? Her small share of offal;
And those three vegetables Britain touts—
Two kinds of cabbage and Brussels sprouts.

Then she'd cycle back to your abode,
That mildewed nest on Charlbury Road,
And then while you shivered beside the grate,
She cooked them on an electric plate.

Oxford those days was pretty grim
Even for those who were in the swim:
The swains of the new Zuleika Dobson
Looked like snively, effete slobs on
Parade when they strutted across the green,
Full of themselves and their Oxford scene,
Their highfalutin winin' and dinin',
Led by dramatic Kenneth Tynan,
Who would learn to criticize one day
The roles that then he tried to play,
Who'd set tongues wagging and hearts aflutter
When he made a fortune on *Oh, Calcutta!*

Rather than listen to their malarkey,
I sat at the feet of Enid Starkie,
Who knew everything there was to know
About Baudelaire and Arthur Rimbaud,
A friend of poets and a friend indeed
Of C. Day Lewis and André Gide.
And on Saturday nights I went to see
Young Dylan Thomas at South Leigh.
Dylan had already mastered the trick
Of wringing the neck of rhetoric.
He'd learned to live and to rejoice
And boomed out in his rich Welsh voice
Lines not Chaucerian or Stuart
But a little quatrain by Gavin Ewart:

"Miss Twye was soaping her breasts in her bath
When she heard behind her a meaning laugh
And to her amazement she discovered
A wicked man in the bathroom cupboard."*
And when the two of them gave up battlin',
I went with Dylan and beautiful Caitlin,
With Dylan as sober as a drunken sailor,
To dine with Margaret and A.J.P. Taylor
In a drawing room built across a stream.
If double pneumonia was your dream,
The place was perfect; a feeble fire
Glowed in the chimney like dead desire,
And around it we gathered to converse
On the state of the world or something worse,
The foibles of some Oxford don.
Caitlin drew near and put a log on;
Then, never pausing to flinch or cough,
A.J.P. Taylor took the log off.
The dampness rose and soaked us through:
Our hearts were gay but our lips were blue.

The days were gray, the encounters cheering
And occasional lectures well worth hearing.
I learned the values of light and dark
In a brilliant series by Kenneth Clark.
Sir Maurice Bowra I also heard,
And Lord David Cecil, the odd bird,
With a sensibility so pure
Some monstrous things he could not endure.
At the BBC when left alone

* "Miss Twye," from *The Collected Ewart, 1933–1980: Poems by Gavin Ewart*
(London: Hutchinson, 1980). © 1980 by Gavin Ewart.

With an enormous microphone,
He found its cold, steel look so trying
And absolutely terrifying
When he tried to speak, not a word could he say
But simply fainted dead away.
Other figures great and small
I met not in the lecture hall
But absorbed their learning and their charms
At the George, the Mitre, and the King's Arms.
To All Souls I went to make my bows
To that Cornish gentleman A. L. Rowse:
And I met without much fuss or planning
Reggie Smith and Olivia Manning.
Remembered, how the faces vary:
Sir John Betjeman and Joyce Cary,
Cyril Connolly, and all—
Good friends Kay and Ernest Stahl,
And what a pleasure it was too be with
Audrey Beacham and Stevie Smith,
And rare indeed the chance to chat
With big Roy Campbell in his broad-brimmed hat.

An English spring was on its way:
On Charlbury Road early one day,
Groping through fog to fetch the coal,
I met my landlady out for a stroll.
She asked, with more concern than wit,
"Spring has arrived: have you seen the great tit?"
A query that in places would stop the traffic,
But she was ornithologic, not pornographic.
(The tit that she meant for me to see
Is like an American chickadee).
But my senses by the fog were blurred.
"Not yet, I haven't," I averred.

Spring did come: when summer followed,
I'd bitten off more than I had swallowed.
I found that my advanced degree
Required not two years' work but three.
The thought of that remote D. Phil.
Made me uneasy, if not ill.
The effort of constant exegesis
Demanded by a doctoral thesis
Gave me nightmares every night.
And so in order that I might write
The poems I knew I had in me,
Oxford I fled for Italy,
Where I could write with force and candor
In the shade of Walter Savage Landor,
Becoming the first Rhodes dropout ever.
But Oxford ties one cannot sever
All that easily even so.
You took the high Rhodes, I, the low.
But I've managed to get on somehow
And write my books—some forty now—
And I've had my little share of fame,
And although I have a common name,
It is far from being a household word.
And yet my vision is unblurred.

Oxford in spirit still remains:
The gray spires lifting from the plains
I see again in my mind's eye,
All the clearer as years go by.
And I'd have you all see them tonight,
Rain-washed in early autumn light,
As limpid and as close to heaven
As when we saw them in forty-seven.

Translations

Harry Martinson: THE FOREST OF CHILDHOOD

Barefoot from tussock to tussock I ran
seeking the farmer's cows,
and saw how the mirrored firmament turned
in the tarn its cloud-tufted wheel.

In the summer forests life played,
and evening was deep with thrushes and heaven high with swallows.
Nothing came of all my dreams and deceits,
but memory enlivens my life
and memories are completed dreams.

To lingonberry patches deep in
summer's own parish
my dream migrates at times
like a crane in spring.

[*from the Swedish*]

Harry Martinson: PEONIES

Summer grew, broadened out;
thickened into positive clumps.
Dark-red farm peonies bulged in the rain.
When they opened their firm-knotted rag balls, she came by,
the lusty queen.
She looked for heavy bouquets,
luxuriant repasts for the senses.
The greenery was wet. Life-wet was the summer-saga:
She had prepared only for life, not for autumn.
Deep in her flesh defiantly she knew
that in time Death would wave to her
with his banner of hay.

[*from the Swedish*]

Harry Martinson: THE HENHOUSE

The hens, arriving early from the day's pickings,
circle a few times around the henhouse floor
and arrange themselves in the current pecking order.
Only when this is made clear
do they leap up to the roost.
Soon they're all seated in rows around the rooster.
He makes a stab or two at sleeping
but there will be no sleep for a while.
The hens fuss and shove.
With peck and cawkle, he must quiet them down.
Then there is a shifting and settling:
one of the hens tries to remember the latest
worm she caught,
but the memory is already fading,
on its way down her crop.
Another hen, on the edge of sleep, recalling clearly
the rooster's prowess, rolls her eyes heavenward,
her fluttering eyelids shutting out the world.

[*from the Swedish*]

Paul Valéry: POMEGRANATES

Pomegranates, fruit whose hard
Rind to rioting seed must yield—
One would think that he beheld
The sundered forehead of a god!

If the heat that you have borne,
O pomegranates opened wide,
Has with the irritant of pride,
Made you crack your ruby walls,

And if your desiccate, golden shell,
From pressure of some hidden force,
Breaks in brilliant gems of juice,

I, at this luminous rupture, turn
My dry thought inward and discern
The architecture of the soul.

[*from the French*]

Jules Laforgue: THE FAR WEST

When they speak of life on the Western Prairie,
My heart leaps up: "That's the place for me!"

To be done with Europe, with religion and law;
There I'll be king, desperado, outlaw.

I will scalp myself of intellect
And paw the ground and genuflect.

Unlettered citizen, one of the gang,
Whipping out Californian slang.

The finest cowboy that ever rode,
A card shark far from the Civil Code.

Between the Pacific and Great Salt Lake
Venison and whiskey: deer-skinned, I'll make

The plains my bed, pure clouds above
Richer than gifts bestowed with love.

And then what? Then pull up stakes, resist
The law, with diamonds as big as your fist,

Play poker at night, in the morning head back
To gather gold nuggets by the sack.

And then, grown old, on a farm settle down
With cows and kids on the edge of town.

And since I can draw, put up if I choose
A sign at the entrance: EXPERT TATTOOS

There you have it. But if my heart
Protests: "Your tribe's lost the art

Of running around," if the eagle's flight
Brings infinity within my sight

Then from such vision the result
Will be my invention of a new cult

That will promote in mystical strains
The Pastoral People of the Great Plains.

How wild are the pictures that postcards display,
And the toys that get broken in our play!

    [*from the French*]

Kjell Hjern:
ON THE GROWTH OF HAIR IN MIDDLE AGE

No poem has yet been written
except possibly in Chinese
about the growth of hair that occurs
during a man's best years
when the hair on his head has begun to thin.

The hair then growing from the nose
can more readily be tolerated
when a man sports a full beard,
but even then it gets in the way
if the cathedral of the nose
has delicate walls.

For this is not just innocent fluff
as on a bald pate
when it tries to deny the aging process.
No, these hairs are like lances,
unfavorably disposed one toward the other.

And when you wish to remove them,
they stick together;
and you are left cursing those miserable tools,
tweezers with warped shanks.

There are, to be sure, bold blades
that seize the nose hairs by the end
and quickly yank them out,
blades that may be compared to those
that operate farther down to snip out the appendix,
which incidentally, needs to be done but once,
while nose hair returns again and again.

Here Science,
which otherwise horses about,
asking in that self-important way,
"What can I do for you?
May I help you?"
has shamefully failed;
and Poetry,
the pompous winged mare,
patronizingly turns her rump on us
when we attempt to re-create
those wretched scenes of everyday life.

   [*from the Swedish*]

Jean-Max Tixier: WRITING

Speaking so as not to be subdued
Word by word I hold back silence
As a dike holds back the ocean
I define absence
For the one who is absent
My words give flesh
To that which has none

To add nothing new to nothing
Is to deny nothingness
I can walk within myself
Without falling into an abyss
Since I am both the step
And the path it takes
Stone and air bound together
Weighing heavily on day
Rolled up in night

Aiming to express the inexpressible
With all of language
Spread out at my feet
Drunk with finding
Promise in unpromising weed
And burgeoning seed
Where it never
Had a chance to sprout

[*from the French*]

Basho: HAIKU

Visiting the graves
white-haired old men edge along
leaning on their canes

Midnight frost: so cold
I'd willingly borrow that
scarecrow's flimsy shirt

Waves of heat shimmer
one or two inches out there
above the dead grass

Spring is leaving us:
birds weep, and tears make glisten
the glazed eyes of fish

The basis of art:
a rice-planting song sung there
deep in the country

Slender summer grass
all that now remains with us
of warriors' dreams

A pale winter sun,
and on the horse's lean back
my frozen shadow

[*from the Japanese*]

Sándor Weöres: THE LUNATIC CYCLIST

sometimes one whose soul is pure
sees himself as if he might
be some cycling lunatic
as he pedals through the night

he the lunatic evokes
who can neither see nor hear
while the pebbles his wheels flick
are flung twanging through his spokes

wheels that cut into the earth
around him weave a dusty veil
the stars above a lazy herd
sleep in their narrow sky-stall

while the wind soaks up his sweat
and shakes out his bushy hair
the lunatic continues yet
to pedal trough the moonlit air

sometimes one whose soul is pure
sees himself as if he might
be that lunatic cycling there
with mounting fury through the night

as clear to him as bread and wine
mirrored by the light of day
the moon that sprinkles round about
on every side its netted ray

cold the light and cold the wind
that blows the lunatic's hair back
while dust humiliates his wheels
and unvirginal is his track

infinite is the cyclist's track
and the soul that's pure and bright
watches while the lunatic
pedals weeping through the night

[*from the Hungarian*]

Sándor Weöres: BOUNDLESS SPACE

When I was no one yet,
light, clear light,
in the winding brooks
I often slept.

As I almost became someone,
a great force rolled me,
stone, rough stone,
ice-veined, down the slope.

And, finally, I have brightened
to live, flame, naked flame,
in rounded, boundless space,
showing our real country.

[*from the Hungarian*]

The Greatest Wealth

WEDDING SONGS

NOW TOUCH THE AIR SOFTLY

Now touch the air softly,
Step gently. One, two . . .
I'll love you till roses
Are robin's-egg blue;
I'll love you till gravel
Is eaten for bread,
And lemons are orange,
And lavender's red.

Now touch the air softly,
Swing gently the broom.
I'll love you till windows
Are all of a room;
And the table is laid,
And the table is bare,
And the ceiling reposes
On bottomless air.

I'll love you till Heaven
Rips the stars from his coat,
And the Moon rows away in
A glass-bottomed boat;
And Orion steps down
Like a diver below,
And Earth is ablaze,
And Ocean aglow.

So touch the air softly,
And swing the broom high.
We will dust the gray mountains,
And sweep the blue sky;
And I'll love you as long
As the furrow the plow,
As However is Ever,
And Ever is Now.

THE BOUQUET

for Marissa and David

The lovers whom today we praise
Once passed each other on some street
And both then went their separate ways.
Where in the world would they ever meet?

They followed other brides and grooms
To places they'll not soon forget
And dined and danced in distant rooms
And still the two had never met.

But then one day a mutual friend
Sat them down on one divan
And where my story might well end
Is where it really just began.

They talked and talked, and then for months
They were the proverbial happy pair,
And had they chosen still to be
My story would have ended there.

But the groom once profiting by chance,
(Another country—better luck?),
Pursued his would-be bride to France
And there it was that lightning struck.

It was in Paris that he chose
To find if she would share his life
And asked, in simple English prose,
"Will you, sweetheart, be my wife?"

She felt deep-down a tingling shock
And up her spine an icy chill
And in her heart a great hot flash,
And she responded, "Yes, I will."

They stood beneath the Eiffel Tower,
And Paris, at the close of day,
Offered at that magic hour
A very special gilded spray

Of every shade of lighted flower
Which, through the darkening evening air,
Emanated from the tower
And fell upon them then and there
                    In a fabulous bouquet.

And we who come to celebrate
Their union this wedding day
Offer them our deeply felt
And very personal bouquet

Of flowers that of words are made,
That will not wither or decay,
That worm or insect won't invade,
And here in print is meant to stay.

SONG FOR A COUNTRY WEDDING

for Deborah and Marc

We have come in the winter
To this warm country room,
The family and friends
Of the bride and the groom,
To bring them our blessing,
To share in their joy,
And to hope that years passing
The best measures employ
> *To protect their small clearing,*
> *And their love be enduring.*

May the hawk that flies over
These thick-wooded hills,
Where through tangled ground cover
With its cushion of quills
The plump porcupine ambles
And the deer come to browse
While through birches and brambles
Clear cold water flows,
> *Protect their small clearing,*
> *And their love be enduring.*

May the green leaves returning
To rock maples in spring
Catch fire, and, still burning,
Their flaming coat fling
On the lovers when sleeping
To contain the first chill
Of crisp autumn weather
With log fires that will
> *Protect their small clearing,*
> *And their love be enduring.*

May the air that grows colder
Where the glacier has left
Its erratic boulder
Mountain water has cleft,
And the snow then descending
No less clear than their love
Be a white quilt depending
From sheer whiteness above
>   *To protect their small clearing,*
>   *And their love be enduring.*

THE GREATEST WEALTH

for Evita and Gregory

I would have instruments that could express
The captive music of clear mountain streams,
The shafted sunlight and the moon's cold beams,
A keyboard so attuned it could address
The songs recorded by your deepest dreams,
To speak for joy, keep discontent at bay
To wish you well upon your wedding day.

I would have baroque fountains cast in bronze
Where water would enclose with silver veils
Sea creatures half encased in virid scales,
And rising, fall, and rise against green lawns
In crystal iridescent peacock tails
Until each eye is dazzled by the spray
To wish you well upon your wedding day.

I would have pinewoods open to a sky
So spicy clear that you could touch the stars,
Lilacs rain-drenched to smell, and cool sandbars
To lie upon, rare pungent herbs to dry
And, memory compacted, store in jars,
And fireflies in a field of new-mown hay
To wish you well upon your wedding day.

I'd have persimmons picked within a glade
Where pheasant for your table moved among
Cold aromatic grass with berries hung,
Goose liver, pink as baby flesh, inlaid
With truffles that, dissolving, drug the tongue,
With salmon, oysters, wine in sweet array
To wish you well upon your wedding day.

I have only words but words are strong;
For if our senses are a kind of sieve
To filter out the rich life that we live,
Then from such riches words can shape a song
To offer up the joy that I would give
And to you thus the greatest wealth convey
To wish you well upon your wedding day.

Words by the Water

OLD CHEROKEE WOMAN'S SONG

They have taken my land,
they have taken my home;
they have driven me here
to the edge of the water.
Cold is the ground
and cold the red water.
At night the men come
to circle the campground;
they carry tall reeds,
each topped with a feather,
a bright eagle feather
to draw our eyes upward
and bring us all hope
for the bitter long journey.
But for me the reed's broken
and the sky it has fallen
where black storm clouds gather.
Cold is the ground
and cold the red water.
My blood it will mix
with the flowing red water:
they have taken my land,
they have taken my home;
I go now to die
beyond the red water

SONG OF THE DISPOSSESSED

You came across the water,
   like gods you walked ashore;
the fabric of our dreaming
   was the clothing that you wore.

You came with ornament
   far brighter than the sun;
you brought the handsome horse,
   the flashing blade, the gun.

You brought your holy book
   that held a world entire,
a life that never ended;
   and water that was fire.

You said, "We'll live as brothers,
   as brothers we will die;
we'll share the forest carpet
   and the blanket of the sky."

But then when we came near you,
   you said, "Now move away;
you come too close now, brother,
   it's dangerous to stay

so close to one another;
   and you must understand
that we know what is better—
   we'll send you to a land

far richer in the west
        beyond the great brown river
where grass is always green
        and where you'll live forever."

And so you took our country,
        you took our sacred ground,
the birds and beasts we cherished,
        the falling water's sound,

the stag that with his antlers
        breaks the sun-flecked trail,
the mockingbird, the turkey,
        the heron and the quail.

You sent us to this desert,
        this sand, these pitted stones,
where wind rakes through the gully,
        and bares the bison's bones,

where now above this barren earth
        your great bald eagle screams,
that robbed us of our country
        and carried off our dreams

A RATIONAL DEPARTURE

Attention fixed with good Descartes
    On all one thinks, not feels,
I board a train and so depart
    On reason's iron wheels.

I think, therefore I am. Godspeed:
    Mind's engines roar ahead,
But, bawdy world, your kiss is blood,
    And my cup, full and red.

RHETORICAL QUESTION

for George Garrett

I heard a poet in a dream cry out:
"Shall I take Rhetoric calmly in my stride:
Or wring its neck like that of some drunk lout,
And leave it writhing there, washed by the tide? . . .

"Shall I take Life—like laundry—wring it out?
Shall I take Life—that has me by the throat—
And do it in? . . . or calmly live it out?"

His answer was in writing what I wrote.

CATS IN A SUMMER GARDEN

Pontifical proud sleepers in the sun,
    plump cats on wicker chairs with long tails curled
    about your full forequarters, tails that twirled
when late you hunted speckled fish at heaven's edge,
        your privilege
    expires. The workman flock to Willow Run.

The stars disperse, and gardeners commence
    the labors of the early morning hours,
    administer to lush, demanding flowers
and fragile roses that are far from Ispahan
        with watering can
    and garden-shears to keep the jungle hence.

Up, cats! The beds are made, and I for one,
    cannot delay: to live a reasoned life,
    promote concord when there is only strife,
means work, for art is long and life is not a joke.
        Like factory smoke
    you drift away . . . What is there to be done?

TO THE MEMORY OF HUBERT CREEKMORE (1907–1966)

Who died in a taxi on his way to the airport

You did not catch your plane;
The taxi rushed ahead,
But its pursuit was vain:
Zero, the meter read
And then your heart stopped dead,
And you did not reach Spain.
You who, living, said
So many things so well,
Things proper, clear, and plain,
Your presence haunts us here,
Your laughter leaves a stain.
We leave you now to death,
To that imagined Spain,
Whose olive groves, red sands,
And golden high plateaus
Your memory commands;
And send, as if by birds,
Into your gentle hands,
This wreath, these meager words.

A GREEN OASIS

He is the king of a country where it never rains,
and in his slumber hunts the unicorn;
where all the mountain waters mourn
he dreams that he has seen
a woman in a green
oasis bring
pomegranates to the train.
And dreams that he has taken in his hand
that fruit which, risen from the yellow sand,
returns to it a thousand blood-red seeds;
and dreams that water comes to work its spell,
and comb his tilting turret like a shell,
and make a kind of flutelike sound among the reeds.

WOMAN AT THE PIANO

When the tall thin lady started to play
the notes flew up and out and away:
like the pink in her cheeks and her dress's loops
they rose in curves, they rolled in hoops
till the chickens flew out of the chicken coops,
the rooster crowed, the donkey brayed,
and the cat meowed.
                              She raised her hands,
she lifted her feet.

What was she playing?
                              An anthem? A hymn?
Nobody knew, but, oh, it was sweet!

How thin she was, how tall and prim,
                              but, oh, how she played!

Everything in you went loose inside
and the world of a sudden became so wide
and open and joyous and free
the fish came flying out of the sea,
the mountains knelt,
                              the birds went wild.

The lady smiled:

and all you could do was hold on to your seat
and simply say:

"For heaven's sake, lady, play, play!
For heaven's sake,
                    lady,
                              play!"

WORDS BY THE WATER

Beneath the dimming gardens of the sky
That ship, my heart, now rides its anchor chain;
A room is harbor when the world's awry
And life's direction anything but plain.
Still is the wind, and softer still the rain.
Sleep in my arms, my love. O sleep, my love.

Time hangs suspended: with its floating farms,
Its peacock-green and terraced atmosphere,
Now sleep awaits us, love. Lie in my arms;
It is not death but distance that I fear,
Dark is the day, and dangerous the year.
Sleep in my arms, my love. O sleep, my love.

ACKNOWLEDGMENTS

Some of these poems appeared first in the *Hopkins Review,* the *Hudson Review, New Letters, Per Contra,* and the *Raintown Review,* and in the following books: *The World below the Window* (Baltimore: Johns Hopkins University Press, 1998), and *The Cherokee Lottery* (Willimantic, CT: Curbstone Press, 2000); and in *Plain Talk* (New York: Center for Book Arts, 1988), *Collected Translations: Italian, French, Spanish, Portuguese* (St. Paul, MN: New Rivers Press, 1985), *Wild Bouquet: Nature Poems by Harry Martinson,* translated by William Jay Smith and Leif Sjöberg (Kansas City, MO: Bkmk Press, 1985), and Sándor Weöres, *Eternal Moment: Selected Poems* (London: Anvil Press, 1988).

POETRY TITLES IN THE SERIES

John Hollander, *Blue Wine and Other Poems*

Robert Pack, *Waking to My Name: New and Selected Poems*

Philip Dacey, *The Boy under the Bed*

Wyatt Prunty, *The Times Between*

Barry Spacks, *Spacks Street, New and Selected Poems*

Gibbons Ruark, *Keeping Company*

David St. John, *Hush*

Wyatt Prunty, *What Women Know, What Men Believe*

Adrien Stoutenberg, *Land of Superior Mirages: New and Selected Poems*

John Hollander, *In Time and Place*

Charles Martin, *Steal the Bacon*

John Bricuth, *The Heisenberg Variations*

Tom Disch, *Yes, Let's: New and Selected Poems*

Wyatt Prunty, *Balance as Belief*

Tom Disch, *Dark Verses and Light*

Thomas Carper, *Fiddle Lane*

Emily Gr

X. J. Ker

Wyatt P

Robert

Vicki H

Timoth

Josephi

Thoma

John B

Charle

Wyatt

Willia

Wyatt

Robert

X. J. K

John T

John B

Rober

Danie

X. J. K

Willia

kins Poetry Series

007